R is for Rhyme

A Poetry Alphabet

Written by Judy Young and Illustrated by Victor Juhasz

Sleeping Bear Press™

315 E. Eisenhower Parkway, Suite 200
Ann Arbor MI 48103
www.sleepingbearpress.com

© 2006 Sleeping Bear Press is an imprint of Gale, a part of Cengage Learning.

10 9 8 7 6 5 4 3 (case)
10 9 8 7 6 5 4 3 2 1 (pbk)

Library of Congress Cataloging-in-Publication Data

Young, Judy.
R is for rhyme : a poetry alphabet / written by Judy Young;
illustrated by Victor Juhasz.
p. cm.
Summary: "From acrostics and ballads to meter and metaphor, author and poet
Judy Young has written a collection of poems to illustrate poetic tools, terms, and
techniques. Each term or technique is demonstrated in an accompanying poem
so readers can see the method at work"—Provided by publisher.
ISBN 978-1-58536-240-0 (case)
ISBN 978-1-58536-519-7 (pbk)
1. Children's poetry, American. 2. Poetry—Authorship—Juvenile literature.
3. Poetics—Terminology—Juvenile literature. I. Juhasz, Victor. II. Title. –
PS3625.O9654R15 2006
811'.6—dc22   2005027794

Printed by China Translation & Printing Services Limited, Guangdong Province, China
Hardcover 3rd Printing / Softcover 1st Printing. 12/2009.

For Lisa Hunter, an excellent teacher and friend.
Thanks for sharing your third graders for poetry time.

JUDY

∽

For Terri, whose smile is my daily poem.

VICTOR

In an acrostic poem, the title is the subject of the poem. It is usually only one or two words long. Each letter of the title starts a line of the poem. The title word is therefore written vertically (up and down) as the first letter of each line. Look at the first letters in each line of "Drawing." Do you see the word "drawing" spelled out? Lewis Carroll included an acrostic, using the name of ten-year-old Alice Pleasance Liddell, in *Through the Looking Glass*.

There are many words that mean almost the same thing as another word. These words are called synonyms. For instance, *big, large, huge, gigantic,* and *enormous* are all synonyms. You can look up words in a book called a thesaurus to find synonyms.

Read "Drawing" again. What word is used to show that imaginations are "captured" with a crayon?

A is for Acrostic

"Drawing"

Delightful pictures
Released onto paper
As
Wild
Imaginations are
Netted with the
Grasp of a crayon.

B is for Ballad

"Ballad of the Butterfly and Rose"

In early days of summer, came
A lovely butterfly.
His wings were painted with the hues
Of sunsets in the sky.

He flew around the garden's blooms,
However, what he chose
To land on was a tiny bud,
The smallest unborn rose.

He stayed there with the bud for weeks
Until it opened wide
And petals colored like the sun
Were waiting there inside.

The butterfly danced for his rose,
The rose collected dew,
A drink to give her butterfly,
And each day their love grew.

One evening under brilliant skies,
Bright yellow, orange, and red,
The butterfly and lovely rose,
Together, they were wed.

Soon summer passed and came the time
When roses start to fade
And butterflies leave for the south,
Yet, knowing that, he stayed.

The butterfly felt freezing winds
But would not leave his bride
And with his wings wrapped round his rose,
Together they both died.

Long ago, storytellers, who traveled from town to town, were the primary source of news, education, and entertainment. Often, they told their tales in poetry forms called ballads. Traditionally, ballads were love stories that ended in tragedy. Many ballads have been put to music and sung. Henry Wadsworth Longfellow wrote the well-known ballad "The Village Blacksmith." Stephen Vincent Benét and Robert Service also wrote ballads.

Ballads are written in groups of four lines. These groups are called stanzas. In each stanza, the last words in the second and fourth lines rhyme. Can you find the rhyming words in each stanza?

Poems often have a specific rhythm called meter. Meter is made of patterns of unstressed and stressed syllables. Each unit of the pattern is called a "foot." In a ballad there are four feet, or beat patterns, in the first and third lines. There are only three feet in the second and fourth lines. Can you hear the meter when you read "Ballad of the Butterfly and Rose" aloud?

Why didn't the butterfly go south for the winter?

Bb

C is for Cinquain

"My Shadow"

Always
Attached to me,
This black transparency.
I can't escape the shape of my
Shadow.

A cinquain (sing-KANE) is any poem or stanza that has five lines. A poet named Adelaide Crapsey developed a type of cinquain poem based on Japanese poetry styles. A Crapsey cinquain has a syllable count of 2-4-6-8-2 syllables per line.

A Crapsey cinquain may or may not rhyme. In "My Shadow," the poet chose to have the second and third lines rhyme. There are also two words inside the fourth line that rhyme. Can you find them? When two words in the same line rhyme, it is called internal rhyme.

When reading a poem, read it like you would read any other kind of writing. Instead of stopping when you come to the end of a line, follow the punctuation, pausing at commas and periods. Some lines do not end with a complete thought. The thought continues onto the next line. That is called enjambment. A good example of enjambment is how the fourth line contines onto the fifth line in "My Shadow."

You can see through a shadow. What are some other things that are transparent?

D is for Doublet

"Rain to Snow"

Rain falls
Leaving the clouds that raid the sky.
They said the day would be gray.
I slid my hands in my pockets,
Walking carefully not to slip in puddles
Or slop mud on my pants.
Then, in a magical moment, the drops began to slow and I watched
As from dripping to drifting, rain changed to snow.

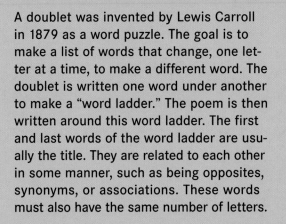

A doublet was invented by Lewis Carroll in 1879 as a word puzzle. The goal is to make a list of words that change, one letter at a time, to make a different word. The doublet is written one word under another to make a "word ladder." The poem is then written around this word ladder. The first and last words of the word ladder are usually the title. They are related to each other in some manner, such as being opposites, synonyms, or associations. These words must also have the same number of letters.

Look at "Rain to Snow." The first word of the doublet is "rain." Look directly under the word "rain" and you will see "raid." The letter "n" in "rain" was changed to a "d" to make "raid." What letter changes next? What new word does it make? Do you see the list of eight words that change one letter at a time until "rain" finally changes to "snow"?

Have you ever been outside when rain changed to snow?

D d

E e

End rhyme means that the last word on one line of a poem rhymes with the last word on another line. Sometimes the rhyming lines are next to each other, sometimes they skip lines. The way in which a poem's lines rhyme makes a rhyming pattern.

There are many rhyming patterns in poetry and some types of poems require a certain pattern. To describe rhyming patterns, letters are assigned to lines. Lines that rhyme with each other are given the same letter. Lines that have a different rhyme are given another letter. Once a rhyming pattern is started, it usually continues throughout the poem.

For example, in "How Would You Act?" there is an *aabb* rhyming pattern. The *aa* tells that the first two lines rhyme at the end. The *bb* tells that the next two lines rhyme with a different rhyming family. That *aabb* rhyming pattern continues throughout each stanza of the poem.

Some of the masters of rhyming poetry include Eugene Field, Robert Frost, Walter de la Mare, Edna St. Vincent Millay, and Robert Louis Stevenson.

E is for End Rhyme

"How Would You Act?"

If you were a bird,
You'd want to be heard.
If you were a horse,
You'd run, of course.

Through water you'd swish
If you were a fish
And if you were an eel
All slimy you'd feel.

A cold-blooded lizard
Would stay out of a blizzard
And a sneaky old fox
Would stalk hens and cocks.

A cat would have fun
Lying out in the sun
And if you were a worm
Through the earth you would squirm.

You see, it's a fact
That however you act
Depends on your kind,
Which brings to my mind,

If you are a child
Should you be wild?

F is for Free Verse

"White Rabbits with Red Wings"

White rabbits with red wings
Flew through my childhood dreams,
Fluttering around the swing in the mulberry tree
And through the peach trees and the plum.

They sat with me in the sycamore,
Feet dangling high above the ground,
Wondering where clouds go on summer days,

And listened for the train,
Running with me through the gap in the hedge
To wave at the man in the caboose
Who went to faraway places.

White rabbits with red wings
Blew dandelion heads,
Drifting with the feathery fluff,
And followed butterflies
Where they floated out of sight.

White rabbits with red wings
Danced upward with the fireflies
Until they blended with the stars,

Leaving me where I stood,
Gazing in a reflecting pool at the summer moon
And wishing on a faraway star
To be a white rabbit
With red wings.

Modern free verse began with Walt Whitman's *Leaves of Grass*. Others who are known for their free verse poetry are Carl Sandburg, Langston Hughes, e.e. cummings, and William Carlos Williams. In free verse poetry there are no rules; no specific rhyming pattern, syllable count, metric pattern, line arrangement, or theme. The poet is "free" to write however he wants.

In free verse, the poet must choose where to "break" the lines in the poem. A "line break" is where one line stops and another begins. A poet may break a line at the end of a complete thought or divide a thought onto different lines. Walt Whitman wrote long lines of free verse. William Carlos Williams's lines were often very short. Some poems have just one word on a line.

Read the poem again. The poet uses imaginary rabbits to symbolize what the child dreams about doing. The wings let the rabbits go places rabbits can't usually go. Where did they go? What other things went places? Why did the child wish to be a white rabbit with red wings?

F f

G is for Ghazal

"My Baby Brother"

When he was little, he wriggled his toes,
Wrinkled his forehead, wrinkled his nose.

He wiggled his fingers and stuck out his tongue,
His arms flapped like wings, his kicking feet rose.

He turned on his stomach, he turned on his back,
All the time laughing with each silly pose.

My mom thought it funny, the camera came out,
And then with a click, each wiggle froze.

Now many years later, when pictures come out,
My dear brother's face turns bright as a rose.

Embarrassed, he wants to toss out these shots
That show a young baby who's not wearing clothes!

A ghazal (GUH-zle) is an ancient Persian poetry form dating back to 1000 BC. It continues to be written widely in Iran, Iraq, and India. In English, Jim Harrison and Adrienne Rich are known for ghazals.

A ghazal has between five and twelve couplets (stanzas with two lines). The second line of each couplet rhymes with the first line of the poem. The rhyming pattern is written *aa ba ca da*, etc.

The last couplet contains the poet's name. Some names are easy because they mean something. Can you find the poet's last name in "My Baby Brother"? Other names are more difficult. However, names can be used as an actual name in the poem. For example, if the poet's name was Davis, the last line of "My Baby Brother" could be "That show baby Davis who's not wearing clothes." The name can also be broken apart. The last line could have been written, "For in the la**st one**, the baby has no clothes," if the poet was named Stone. Write a ghazal using your name!

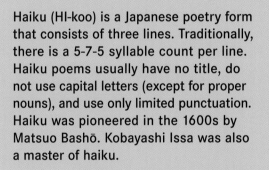

H is for Haiku

pearly triangles
flash in the hot noonday sun
a crocodile yawns

Haiku (HI-koo) is a Japanese poetry form that consists of three lines. Traditionally, there is a 5-7-5 syllable count per line. Haiku poems usually have no title, do not use capital letters (except for proper nouns), and use only limited punctuation. Haiku was pioneered in the 1600s by Matsuo Bashō. Kobayashi Issa was also a master of haiku.

Although haiku poems are very short, they traditionally have four main elements. Imagery is a major component of haiku. Imagery refers to the use of words to "paint" an image, "showing" you a picture you can see in your mind. Haiku also suggests a season and makes observations about nature. Finally, there is an element of surprise in this picture drawn with words, making you "see" something that you are not expecting. Were you expecting a crocodile to yawn? What season is suggested in this haiku?

Another Japanese poetry style similar to haiku is senryu (SEN-ree-you). The senryu also has 5-7-5 syllable count, but tends to be about humans or man-made topics rather than nature.

Poems often have a rhythm or a beat. The rhythmical beat is called meter and is measured in "feet." A foot is made up of a pattern of stressed and unstressed syllables.

The most common meter in English poetry is iambic (eye-AM-bick). It is made up of "iambs" (EYE-ams). An iamb is two syllables long. The first syllable is unstressed. The second syllable is stressed. For example, look at the second line of "Two Chains." It is divided up into four iambs. You would say that the line has four feet. The lowercase letters are unstressed. The uppercase letters are stressed.

to SEE / if HE / could FIND / a TREAT

Read "Two Chains" aloud. Do you hear the rhythm of the iambic meter? The sonnets of William Shakespeare, Elizabeth Barrett Browning, and Christina Rossetti are written in iambic meter.

Sometimes titles are chosen to help the reader look at a poem in a different way. Think about the title "Two Chains." One chain is the chain of events that happen. What is the other chain?

I is for Iambic

"Two Chains"

A dragonfly flew by the pond
To see if he could find a treat.
He landed on a floating leaf
And looked for little bugs to eat.

It didn't see the frog that sat
Upon a mossy rock so still
That thought the dragonfly might make
A very, very tasty meal.

Behind the frog there lay a snake
Who slithered quickly toward his prey
And in a tree there stood a hawk
Who thought a snake would make his day.

Now when a cow that eats just grass
Stepped in the pond to drink that day
A ripple moved the leaf and scared
The hungry dragonfly away.

The frog jumped in, the snake crept off,
The mighty hawk took to the sky
And so their chance to have a feast,
Came to an end and passed them by.

The cow stepped out to eat more grass,
But never even had a hunch,
That she became the only one
Who got the chance to eat her lunch.

A jingle is a simple, catchy poem about a light or humorous subject. Jingles use rhyme, rhythm, and repeating words or lines to make the poem easy to remember. Because the sound of the words makes the poem likely to attract attention, jingles are often put to music and used in television and radio commercials. The use of repetition, rhyme, and rhythm gets the jingle "stuck in your mind," which is what advertisers want.

There are three major parts of a jingle written for commercials. The verse tells the details, facts, or gives a story. The tag is the name of the company or product. It is repeated several times throughout the jingle. The hook tells why you want or need the product.

Read the jingle. The verse lists kinds of candy. The tag names the store, and the hook tells you it's the sweetest place to stop. When you think about candy, "The Sweet Tooth Candy Shop" hopes their jingle will pop into your mind and you will come to their shop to spend your money!

Jj

J is for Jingle

"The Sweet Tooth Candy Shop"

Taffy, suckers, and lollipops,
Lemon, lime, and orange gumdrops,
At the Sweet Tooth Candy Shop,
It's the sweetest place to stop!

Peppermint sticks and chocolate bars,
Drive right up here in your car
To the Sweet Tooth Candy Shop,
It's the sweetest place to stop!

Is candy what you like to eat?
Then you will find all sorts of sweets
At the Sweet Tooth Candy Shop,
It's the sweetest place to stop!

K is for Kyrielle

"Oh, Don't You Wish"

To swim with dolphins or with whales,
Fly in space on a comet's tail,
Or float in bubbles, golden blue,
Oh, don't you wish your dreams were true?

To play with animals that talk,
Through magic kingdoms take a walk,
Or have a fairy tickle you,
Oh, don't you wish your dreams were true?

To soar like eagles, wings spread wide,
Or down a crystal mountain slide,
Each morning when you wake anew,
Oh, don't you wish your dreams were true?

The kyrielle (keer-ee-EL) is an old French poetry form. Each stanza in a kyrielle has four lines, and each line has eight syllables. The last line of the first stanza repeats itself as the last line of all the other stanzas. This repeating line is called a refrain. In John Payne's famous "Kyrielle," he repeats the line "All things must end that have begun."

The kyrielle also uses a specific rhyming pattern. Remember, when describing a rhyming pattern, letters are assigned to the lines to show which ones rhyme with each other. When writing the letters to show the rhyming pattern in a poem with repeating lines, a capital letter is used to show that a line repeats itself from one stanza to the next. Therefore, the rhyming pattern for "Oh, Don't You Wish" is *aabB*. The capital "B" tells that each stanza has the same last line. Some kyrielles use an *abaB* rhyming pattern.

Read the poem again. What dreams have you had that you wish would come true?

A limerick is a five-line poem which uses rhyme and humor. The first line usually names a person or the place where a person is from. It often starts with something like "There once was a person named..." or "There once was a person from...." The next lines tell something about that person, what he is like, or what he has done. The last line sums up the person or his activities in a humorous manner. Edward Lear and Ogden Nash are both well known for this humorous poetry style.

Limericks use an *aabba* rhyming pattern. The limerick also uses a specific metric pattern. Lines 1, 2, and 5 have three metric feet (stress patterns) and lines 3 and 4 are shorter, with two feet.

A thesaurus is a useful tool for poets. It helps find words that mean about the same thing as another word. In "The Ballerina," the word "frau" is another word for "woman." It rhymes with "how" and "now." What word rhymes with "frau" in "The Ballerina"?

L₁

L is for Limerick

"The Ballerina"

There once was a hippo named Rose
Who thought she had delicate toes
But on stage, the old frau
Would not take a bow
For her tutu was tight, I suppose.

M m

"Bluebird"

A piece of summer sky
With a bit of sunrise on his breast
Landed in the birdbath,
Scattering diamonds
Which glistened in the air
And glittered the rainbow of colors
In the garden below.

The use of metaphor (MET-a-for) is an important tool for poets. A metaphor compares something by saying it is an entirely different thing. However, there is a common thread between the two things the metaphor is comparing.

For example, in "Bluebird," the poem says "a piece of summer sky" landed in the bird-bath. It really wasn't a piece of sky, it was really a bluebird. Because the bird and sky are both blue, this metaphor "shows" you how blue the bird is. It doesn't just "tell" you that it is blue. There are several metaphors in "Bluebird." Can you find them?

Another poetic tool is a simile (SIM-a-lee). It is related to the metaphor. However, instead of saying "something IS something else," the simile says "something IS LIKE something else." A metaphor says a bluebird IS a piece of summer sky. A simile says a bluebird is LIKE a piece of summer sky.

Emily Dickinson frequently used metaphors, such as calling a daffodil a yellow bonnet. Can you find metaphors and similes in other poems in this book?

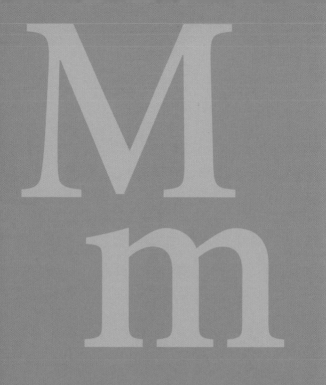

A narrative poem is any poem that tells a story. Narrative poems can use meter and rhyme, such as in a ballad, or can be written in free verse. Originally, narrative poems were recited, in oral tradition, by bards who sometimes changed the poems from one telling to the next. Often, several versions of the same poem survived to written form.

A very long, book-length narrative poem, such as Homer's *The Odyssey*, is called an epic poem. Traditionally, epic poems relate the history, myths, and beliefs of a culture. *John Brown's Body*, by Stephen Vincent Benét, is an epic poem about America's Civil War.

Some narrative poems have someone speaking in them. This is called dialogue. Do you see the dialogue in "Reading Homer"? The words inside the quotation marks are what the teacher said. Has your teacher ever suggested you read a particular poem or book?

Robert Frost wrote many narrative poems, including "A Girl's Garden" and "Stopping by Woods on a Snowy Evening." Can you find five other narrative poems in this book?

N is for Narrative

"Reading Homer"

My teacher said that I must read
Stuff by this Homer guy.
"Just open up your book," she said,
"Give him a little try."

I didn't think I'd like the poem
He wrote so long ago,
But when I started reading it
I couldn't stop, you know!

He wrote of this Odysseus dude
Who, sailing home from Troy,
Ticked off the great god of the sea
Because he harmed his boy.

His boy happened out to be
A giant with one eye
Who ate the sailors of the ship
Like they were apple pie.

Odysseus stabbed him in the eye,
Escaping from his wrath,
But more disastrous adventures would
Await him on his path.

Like Sirens singing soothing songs
That lured men to their graves,
A witch that turned men into pigs,
And storms with raging waves.

I couldn't wait to turn each page
To see what else I'd find,
And daydreams of Odysseus now
Completely fill my mind.

O is for Onomatopoeia

"The Ears of an Elephant"

If you had the ears of an elephant,
You might hear the bugs that crunch
On leaves that whisper whooshing words
As they're gobbled up for lunch.

You might hear the snap of butterflies
As they open up their wings,
Like a sail that catches up the wind
On a day when sunshine sings.

You might hear the sizzle of a drop
Of rain that hits hot sand
Or the cacophonous crash and clatter
As the snowflakes gently land.

If you had the ears of an elephant,
You might hear the crispy calls
And sounds that whir and buzz and plop
From things both great and small.

Onomatopoeia (ON-uh-MAH-tuh-PEE-uh) is another tool that poets use. It refers to words that sound like the noise the word makes. For example, if you drop a pan, you may say it "bangs" on the floor. The word "bang" sounds like the noise made by the pan hitting the floor. Words like *crunch*, *hiss*, *roar*, and *splat* are onomatopoetic (ON-uh-MAH-tuh-po-ET-ik) words.

There are two kinds of onomatopoetic words. Euphonic (YOU-fon-ik) words sound soft and smooth, such as *whoosh*, *hiss*, and *puff*. Cacophonous (kuh-KAH-fon-is) words sound hard, hoarse, and rough, such as *clatter*, *crunch*, and *clank*.

Can you find examples of onomatopoeia in "The Ears of An Elephant"? Which are euphonic words? Which are cacophonous words? Edgar Allan Poe used onomatopoeia in "The Bells," to make you "hear" different types of bells ringing.

What are some other small sounds you may hear if you had the ears of an elephant?

P p

P is for Picture Poem

"The Kite"

Picture poems are meant to not only be read, but also be seen. In a picture poem, the words are arranged on the page to look like the subject of the poem. The shape, font, letter size, color, and positioning of the words on the page are all tools the poet uses when writing picture poems. Some picture poems are shaped like an item, as in "A Kite." Others show an action by following the line of words. For example, the following tells you where you would go if you

dove off a d i
                v
                 i
                  n
                   g
                    b o a r d.

Picture poems are also called calligrams, concrete, or shaped poems. They may be written in rhymed and metered verse, or in free verse. George Herbert wrote some shaped poetry in the 1600s. However, Guillaume Apollinaire is often referred to as the inventor of picture poems in the early 1900s.

A
high flying
acrobat, I flutter
in the breeze, way up
with the clouds, above all the
trees. I'm a bright shooting star,
a rainbow with sails, or maybe
a dragon with a long curvy
tail. When there is   a
March wind hang
on tight to me, I
decorate skies,
look up and
you'll
see!

Hang on tight, hang on tight, if you let go,

My tail keeps me smooth and steady. Let me fly when you are ready.

I   I
dip   dip
and I   and I
twist and twist
and I   and I
dip   dip
I   I

I   I
dip   dip
and I   and I
twist and twist
and I   and I
dip   dip
I   I

of sight. Hang on tight, hang on tight, if you let go,

Stanzas are lines of poetry that are grouped together. Quatrain is the name for stanzas that are four lines long. Many poetic structures require that they be written in quatrains. How many quatrains does "My Quilt" have? Can you find other poems in this book that are written in quatrains?

Stanzas can be any length. A poem can be written in one large stanza or it can be divided up into shorter stanzas. There are special names for stanzas that are different lengths. The names for these stanzas are listed below. Look at the list. How many lines are there in stanzas called "couplets"? Can you find a poem in this book that is written in couplets?

monostich - 1 line stanza
couplet   - 2 line stanza
tercet   - 3 line stanza
quatrain   - 4 line stanza
cinquain   - 5 line stanza
sestet   - 6 line stanza
septet   - 7 line stanza
octave   - 8 line stanza

Read "My Quilt" again. Do you have anything that holds special memories for you? Write a poem about it!

Q is for Quatrain

"My Quilt"

My grandmother made
The quilt on my bed,
With squares made of memories
And colorful thread.

This pink square was cut
From the first dress I wore,
The yellow square came from
Some pants that I tore.

I wore this square fishing,
And that to the zoo,
To the park I wore red,
To first grade I wore blue.

My quilt is so special
That's no mystery,
Each night I sleep tight
With my own history.

R is for Rap

"Cowboy Rap"

I wanna be a cowboy, I wanna ride a horse,
So I went to the boss man and I told him this of course.
He asked me could I ride, and he asked me other things,
But the last thing that he asked me is he asked me could I sing.

I gave a little smile and a yippee yippee yea,
And the boss man said I'd do, and he hired me right away.
He told me cows are restless when night is dark and deep,
And said that it was up to me to sing them cows to sleep.

We rode across the prairie, we rode the whole day long,
And sittin' in the saddle, I thought up my sweet song.
And when the stars came out, with my lasso 'cross my lap,
I rode out with them cows and I started up my rap.

With a scritch,
And a scratch,
And loud noises by the batch,
I called out to them cows,
All you mammas hear me now!
Chew your cud,
In the mud,
Don't you worry 'bout no thing,
Swing your cute,
Little tails,
To the rhythm that I sing.

All them cows started mooin', I thought they liked my lead,
But the next thing I knew, they had started to stampede.
The boss man, he was angry, he said "Son, you're gonna change.
Tomorrow when you sing, just sing home, home on the range!"

Rap is a style of vocal music with its roots traced to jazz poetry. It is known for its strong rhythmic beat, often combined with rhyming couplets, and is usually chanted (performed) aloud. The style is used to express a wide range of themes. Rap poetry has even been used in commercials.

Cowboy poetry emphasizes the history and folklore associated with the West. Originally, cowboys reciting poems about their life on the range passed these poems from campfire to campfire. In 1886 Lysius Gough became the first Texas cowboy to publish a book of cowboy poetry. Traditionally, cowboy poetry is rhymed and metered verse, following a ballad form that tells a story. Today, cowboy poetry is written in many styles.

Sometimes it is fun to combine types of poetry. In "Cowboy Rap," the poet had fun mixing the western ranch, storytelling theme of cowboy poetry with the rhythm of rap.

A sonnet is a complex poetry form that follows many rules. A sonnet has fourteen lines. Each line is written in iambic pentameter. Remember, an iambic foot is a set of two syllables: an unstressed syllable followed by a stressed syllable. Pentameter (pen-TAM-a-ter) means there are five feet per line (or five sets of unstressed/stressed syllables).

There are several traditional styles of sonnets, but two are used the most. The style is based on the rhyming pattern and named after the poets who developed the pattern, William Shakespeare and Francesco Petrarch. "Yellow Dog" is a Shakespearean, or English, sonnet. It has a rhyme pattern of *abab cdcd efef gg*. A Petrarchan, or Italian, sonnet has a rhyming pattern of *abba abba cdc dcd*.

Sonnets can be written about any subject matter but traditionally are about love. An experience or problem is set up in the first eight lines. Then there is a change in events and the problem is solved in the last six lines. What was the problem in "Yellow Dog," and how did it end up?

S is for Sonnet

"Yellow Dog"

I went out to the barn one wintry night
To shut the doors the wind had opened wide.
I was surprised to see by lantern light
A yellow dog was sitting there inside.

I did not know her, nor did she know me,
And if I got too close she raised her fur,
But she was hungry, it was plain to see,
And gobbled up the food I offered her.

Those wintry days, she would not let me near,
But as spring rains began to thaw the ground,
She licked my hand and let me scratch her ears
And by my side, she followed me around.

And now upon my feet she lays her head
And sleeps each night on pillows by my bed.

T is for Tanka

waxy hexagons
dripping with oozy nectar
sealed in vaulted hives
be careful of stinging swords
guarding a golden treasure

A tanka (TONG-kah) is a Japanese poetry form with a count of 5-7-5-7-7 syllables per line. As with the haiku, the imagery of nature is a major subject of a tanka. However, a tanka often combines nature with human concerns. A tanka is also called a waka or uta.

The tanka is older than haiku. The first three lines of the tanka, called hokku, was written as an image that had been observed. The last two lines, called a renga, was an answer or response to that image. Often, poets had "renga parties." Poets would write a hokku on the way to the party and then trade them with another poet, who would write the two renga lines. Much later in time, the hokku became acknowledged for its own special qualities and was published as haiku.

Tankas have been written by many Japanese poets for over a thousand years. Masaoka Shiki and Yosano Akiko preserved the tanka in modern literature.

What image do you picture with this tanka's stinging swords and golden treasure?

U is for Ubi Sunt

"Extinction"

Where did all the great auks go,
And dodos and lava mice, too?
What happened to Tasmanian tigers?
I haven't seen them, have you?

Where did the passenger pigeons go,
That once populated the sky?
And where went the Yunnan box turtle?
Why did these creatures all die?

Will someday we ask where the whale is?
Will we wonder where rhinos once ran?
Will there be whooping cranes and bald eagles?
The answer depends upon man.

Ubi sunt (OO-BEE sunt) means "where are" in Latin. Ubi sunt poems originated because of an ancient custom of calling out a list of the names of the dead and missing after a battle. In early ubi sunt poems, poets asked what happened to certain groups of people. Other ubi sunt poetry named spirits or muses, asking them where they were when a person died, and why hadn't they protected that person. Today, ubi sunt poems may begin by asking where a list of sports figures or heroes, or maybe just friends or ancestors, have gone. Some ubi sunt poems start by wondering what happened to certain places or times.

French poet François Villon wrote several famous ubi sunt poems. His most famous asks "where are the snows of yester-year?" Pete Seeger wrote an ubi sunt poem for the lyrics of his famous folk song that asks "where have all the flowers gone?"

Sometimes poems are written to make a statement about important social issues. What issue is the poet concerned about in "Extinction"?

U u

V is for Villanelle

"The Rule"

At my house it was the rule
To do my homework everyday
When I got home from school.

I'd sit upon the kitchen stool
And get my work done right away;
At my house it was the rule.

My mother, she was not a fool.
She caught me if I went to play
When I got home from school.

She said, "Don't be a stubborn mule,
Get busy and don't disobey!"
At my house it was the rule.

I always thought it would be cool
To play like it was Saturday
When I got home from school.

"It may seem strict, but if you study you'll
Get better grades," my mom would say.
At my house it was the rule
When I got home from school.

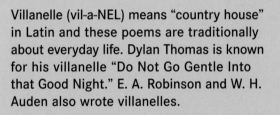

Villanelle (vil-a-NEL) means "country house" in Latin and these poems are traditionally about everyday life. Dylan Thomas is known for his villanelle "Do Not Go Gentle Into that Good Night." E. A. Robinson and W. H. Auden also wrote villanelles.

Villanelles have nineteen lines, divided into six stanzas. The first five stanzas have three lines and the last stanza has four. In a villanelle, all the first and third lines rhyme with each other and all the second lines rhyme together.

Read "The Rule." Did you notice some lines are repeated? In a villanelle, the first line of the poem is repeated as the last line in the second and fourth stanzas. The third line of the poem is repeated as the last line in the third and fifth stanzas. Then, both of these lines are repeated as the last two lines of the poem. Confusing? Yes, but if you look carefully at "The Rule," you will be able to see the rhyming and line repetition patterns.

What is the rule for doing homework at your house?

Words that "almost" rhyme are called weak rhymes. Say the last words in each pair of lines in "My Song." Do you hear that they do not exactly rhyme, but they almost do? Weak rhymes are also called slant, off, near, or half rhymes. Another kind of rhyme is a visual rhyme. These words look like they would rhyme but they don't sound at all alike. "Good" and "food" are visual rhymes. Visual rhymes are also called eye rhymes. Read some of Ogden Nash's humorous poetry. He had fun playing with a variety of ways to "make" words rhyme.

How words sound is important when writing poetry. In addition to rhyming words, there are other types of sound combinations that poets purposely use. Alliteration refers to words that start with the same sound, such as "five fidgety fingers." Consonance means that words have the same ending consonant sound, such as "giant elephant print." Assonance occurs when words have the same vowel sounds, such as "pigs knit mittens."

Do you ever do something to irritate somebody? Write a poem about it!

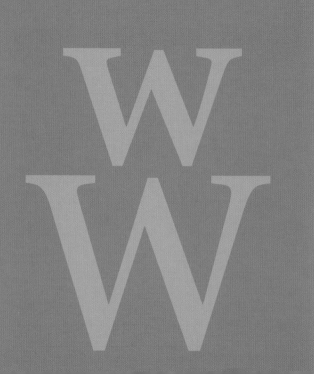

W is for Weak Rhyme

"My Song"

I find that it is very easy
To drive my mom completely crazy.

All I have to do is sing
A song that talks about nothing.

I start to sing when day is young
And make my tune last all day long

For when my song comes to an end,
I start it up all over again.

My mother says she loves me dearly
But when I sing, must I really

Choose that awful song to sing
Instead of one that says something?

X x

A Xanadu (ZAN-a-doo) poem refers to a poem that describes an imaginary place that is more beautiful and more wondrous than any place that really exists.

The word Xanadu comes from a famous poem called "Kubla Khan" by Samuel Taylor Coleridge. Kubla Khan (KOO-bla KAHN) was a real person who conquered China in the eleventh century. In the poem, however, Coleridge made up a beautiful under-ground kingdom and had Kubla Khan visit it. Coleridge called this make-believe kingdom Xanadu. Now, poems that describe a place of unbelievable beauty are called Xanadu poems. William Butler Yeats described his ideal world in "The Lake Isle of Innisfree."

In the poem, "Xanadu," the poet doesn't describe a beautiful place, but wonders how to get to exotic places that other authors have written about. Have you read about any of the kingdoms mentioned in "Xanadu"? What would your Xanadu look like?

X is for Xanadu

"Xanadu"

Where do you go when you want to leave
To visit grander places?
How do you get to these magic worlds
Without leaving any traces?

Dorothy was blown to the land of Oz
And Jack climbed a great beanstalk,
Four children walked through a wardrobe door
To a world where animals talk.

Wendy was sprinkled with fairy dust
And flew with Peter Pan,
Alice was falling down a rabbit hole
When she came to Wonderland.

When I want to go to a magical place,
To a place like Xanadu,
I just open a book and step right in,
I've been everywhere, how 'bout you?

Y is for You Voice

"Hanging On"

You are a leaf,
hanging on to the branch through wind and rain,
hanging on as you turn red,
hanging on until spring releases winter.

You watch as others let go,
you watch as they drop,
but you hang on,
hang on.

Because you want to hang on the longest,
you want to be the very last,
the last to release your grip,
the last to drop.

You want to be the last
to let go of the bar
that's held tight in your fists,
hanging onto the record in P.E.

So, you say to yourself,
you are a leaf,
hang on,
hang on.

Y y

When you read a poem, you can tell who the poem is about by the pronouns that are used. The words *I, you, he, she, it, they,* and *we* are pronouns.

In a "you voice" poem, the poet uses the word "you" to make you feel like you are reading about yourself. The "you voice" tells you what YOU are doing. YOU become the character the poem is about. "You voice" is also called "second person."

Some poems are written in first person, using the pronouns *I* and *we*. First person poems make the poem sound like it is about the poet who wrote the poem. Third person poems, using pronouns *he, she, they,* and *it,* make the poem sound like it is about someone else, not the poet, or the reader. Look at some other poems. What voice or person are they written in?

In "Hanging On," a metaphor is used, saying you are a leaf. What are "you" doing that reminds you of a leaf?

Z is for Zany Words

"Skimble-scamble"

Some poems are filled with zany words
That make you laugh when they are heard.
They look real long and hard to say
But make the poem joke and play.

Sometimes the poet makes words up
Like picklypoo and schnazzlecup
But sometimes these strange words are real
Like wallaroo and glockenspiel.

So if a quidnunc quickly skedaddles
Lickety-split to tell and tattle
That you've written a poem all skimble-scamble
With words where nonsense seems to ramble,

Just tell that little nosy girl
That you like words that swip and flirl
And don't get irky or contrary
If they're not found in a dictionary!

Zany, crazy words make a poem sound playful. Dr. Seuss is famous for making up funny sounding words and Lewis Carroll wrote "Jabberwocky," a poem filled with zany, made-up words. There are also real words that sound zany. These words are fun to use, too. Use a thesaurus and a dictionary to find unusual, zany-sounding words.

In "Skimble-scamble," the words "picklypoo" and "schnazzlecup" are totally made up. The poet played around with real words "flip" and "swirl," trading letters to make two new words, "swip" and "flirl." The letter "y" was also added to the real word "irk," which means to annoy. This made a new word, "irky." These new words are fun but still give the poem a certain feeling.

The title word, "skimble-scamble," is a real word. It means "nonsense." How does the title fit with the poem? Here are some other real words in "Skimble-scamble" that sound zany:

wallaroo: a kind of kangaroo
skedaddle: to leave quickly
glockenspiel: a musical instrument
lickety-split: quickly
quidnunc: a nosy person

Poetry Pointers From Judy Young

Poetry is written to be heard or read. It is the language from the heart, the language used to see, hear, feel, smell, and taste the world. The poet wants to share his or her world. To do this, the poet uses many "tools" when writing a poem. These tools may include different poetry forms, patterns of rhyme or rhythm, and, most important, the very careful selection of words.

R is for Rhyme: A Poetry Alphabet introduces you to many of the tools that a poet uses. As you read about the tool, go back to the poem to see the tool in use. Look for that tool in other poems throughout this book and in other books, as well. Remember, however, that the tools used are not the important part of poetry. Just like a hammer is a tool to build a house, these poetic tools are only used to build a poem. What is important is what the poet has to say, how the poem makes you feel, what the words mean to you. Does the poem make you happy or sad? Does it paint a picture in your mind or tell a story? What connections can you make between the poem and your life? Use what you have learned by writing your own poetry. Experiment with poetic tools. Try new ways to say what you feel and see, to tell the stories you have to tell.

A special note to parents and teachers:

Read poetry aloud to children and encourage them to read poetry for themselves. Read all sorts—long, short, rhyming, nonrhyming, funny, and serious. By doing so, not only do you allow children to see and interpret the world from many directions, you also help them learn and feel the power of words.

Encourage children to write poems. The short format of a poem makes a perfect place to teach different writing conventions. Invite children to experiment with their words, using different tools. Writing poetry helps children develop confidence in writing which spreads to other writing genres. Most importantly, however, poetry writing gives children an outlet for expressing their own interpretations of their world and helps them discover the power and importance of their own words.

Alliteration: a group of words clustered together that have the same first sound ("feathery fluff floats")

Anapestic Meter: a pattern of two unstressed syllables and one stressed syllable (/ in a BOX / un der NEATH / clo set SHELVES/)

Blank Verse: a poem written with meter but not rhyme

Couplet: a two-line stanza

Enjambment: when a phrase doesn't come to a natural pause at the end of a line, but continues onto the next line (the fourth and fifth lines in "My Shadow" is an example of enjambment)

Foot: one unit of a pattern of stressed and unstressed syllables that make up the meter of a poem

Free Verse: poems written without rhyme, meter, or a specific poetic form

Iambic Meter: a pattern of one unstressed and one stressed syllable (/he WENT / to SEE / his MOM/)

Internal Rhyme: when two or more words within one line rhyme

Line: words that are in a horizontal row

Line Break: where a line ends

Metaphor: a comparison that says one thing is something else

Meter: the rhythm made by set patterns of stressed and unstressed syllables

Onomatopoeia: words that sound like the noise they make

Pentameter: pent means "five" so pentameter means five metric feet

Poetic License: when a poet purposely breaks "rules" of grammar, sentence structure, patterns, set forms, etc., we say that the poet has "poetic license" to do so

Quatrain: a four-line stanza

Refrain: a line or lines that are repeated

Rhyme: two or more words that end in the same vowel and consonant sounds

Rhythm: beat

Simile: a comparison using "like" or "as"

Stanza: lines of poetry that are grouped together on the page

Stress: when saying a word, more accent is placed on one syllable than another

Subject: theme of a poem; what the poem is about

Syllable: a part of a word that contains one vowel sound

Synonym: words that have the same, or similar, meaning

Traditional: A specific form, rhyming pattern, metric pattern, or subject that is usually associated with a certain type of poem (sonnets are traditionally about love)

Trochaic Meter: a pattern of one stressed and one unstressed syllable (/UN der / WA ter / LIVES a / MON ster/)

Unstressed: when saying a word, less accent is placed on one syllable than another

Untitled: a poem without a title

Verse: a rhymed and/or metered poem

Visual Imagery: words that seem to "show" you a picture in your mind

Visual Rhyme: words that look like they rhyme, but don't

Weak Rhymes: words that almost rhyme